OUTER LIMITS Z-3 DAZZLING FACES

Dave Lewis

authorHOUSE®

AuthorHouse™
1663 Liberty Drive
Bloomington, IN 47403
www.authorhouse.com
Phone: 1 (800) 839-8640

Published by AuthorHouse 06/02/2017

ISBN: 978-1-5246-9557-6 (sc)
ISBN: 978-1-5246-9568-2 (e)

Print information available on the last page.

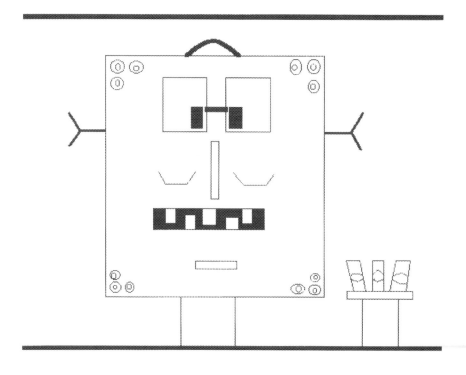

15

16

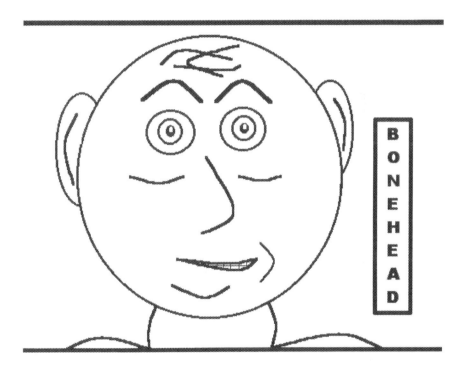

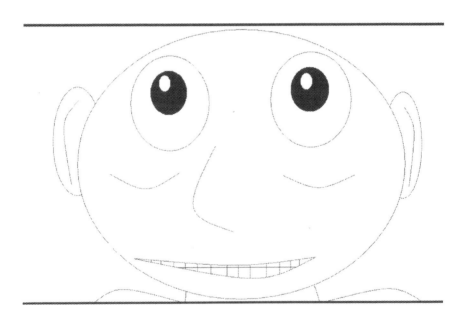

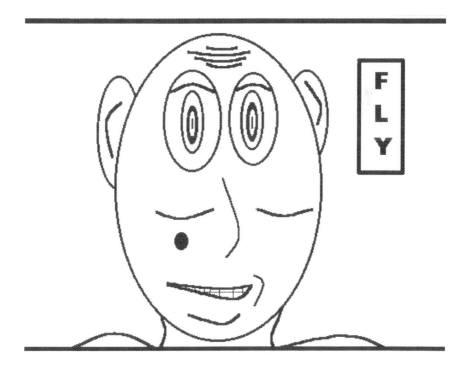

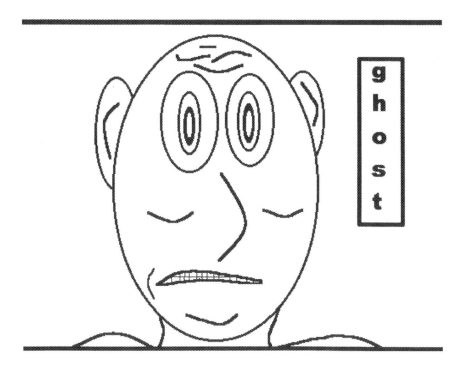

ghost

26

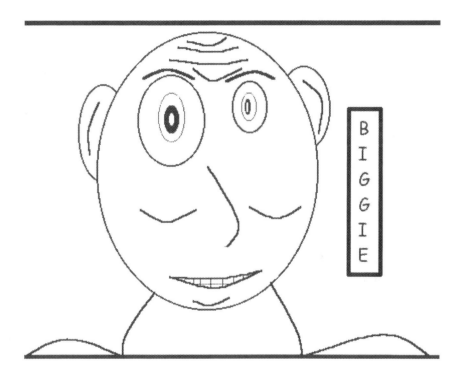

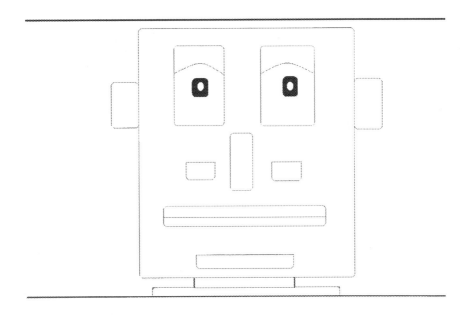

34

35

38

41

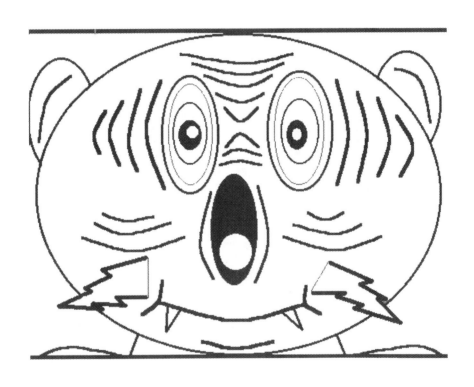

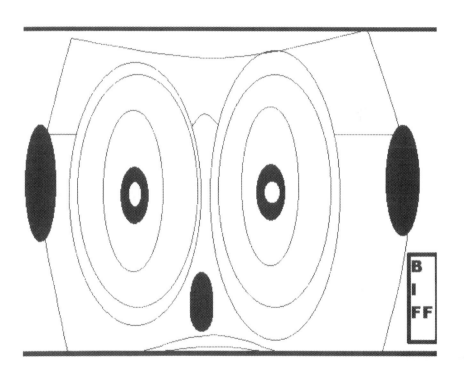

48

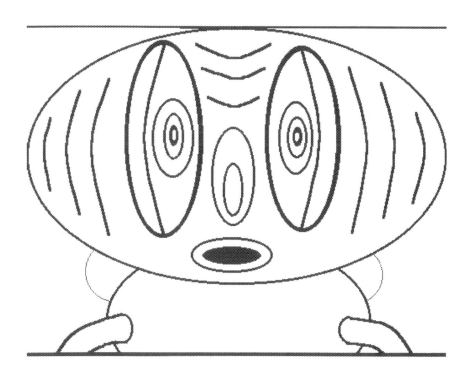

WIZZY

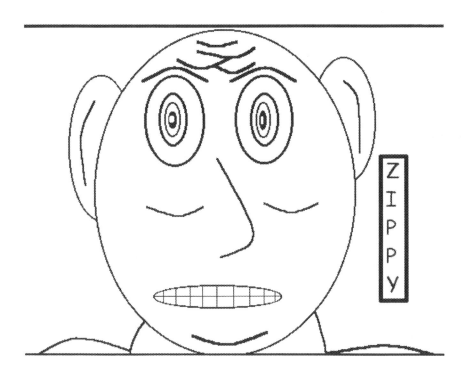

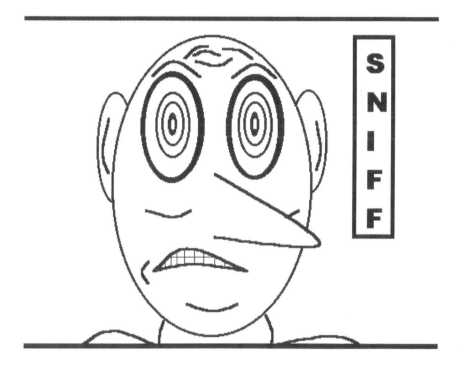

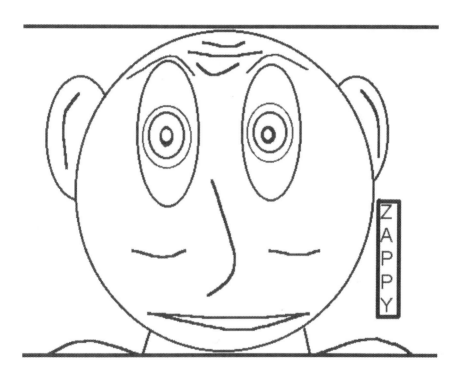

Printed in the United States
By Bookmasters